I0481631

Bitcoin:

Best Strategies for Investing and Profiting from Bitcoin

Mark Clarkson

Table of Contents

Introduction...1

Chapter 1: Bitcoin Background 3

Chapter 2: Getting Started with Bitcoin.......21

Chapter 3: Bitcoin Investing...................... 34

Chapter 4: Bitcoin Trading........................ 54

Conclusion 70

The following eBook is reproduced below with the goal of providing information that is as accurate and reliable as possible. Regardless, purchasing this eBook can be seen as consent to the fact that both the publisher and the author of this book are in no way experts on the topics discussed within and that any recommendations or suggestions that are made herein are for entertainment purposes only. Professionals should be consulted as needed prior to undertaking any of the action endorsed herein.

This declaration is deemed fair and valid by both the American Bar Association and the Committee of Publishers Association and is legally binding throughout the United States.

Introduction

Congratulations on purchasing *Bitcoin: Best Strategies for Investing and Profiting from Bitcoin* and thank you for doing so. With so much talk surrounding the heights that Bitcoin has reached so far, you can be forgiven for thinking the ship has sailed when it comes to making a profit from either investing in it in the long or the short-term. Nothing could be further from the truth, however, and with some analysts anticipating prices as high as $60,000 per unit by the end of 2018, there is no better time to jump in.

To ensure that you hit the ground running, the following chapters will discuss everything you need to know about the history of Bitcoin, how it works, and how it grew to the more than $30 billion market cap it has today. From there you will learn about the things you will need to get started investing successfully, including a Bitcoin wallet and a trustworthy exchange. With that out the way, you will then learn about the many benefits of investing in Bitcoin along with how to maximize your profits via a buy and hold strategy. Finally, you will learn about trading Bitcoin in the short-term along with multiple strategies for doing so successfully.

This book is designed to give you clear and thorough information about Bitcoin. There are plenty of books on this subject on the market, thanks again for choosing this one! Every effort was made to ensure it is full of as much useful information as possible. Please enjoy!

Chapter 1: Bitcoin Background

With the cryptocurrency price explosion that took place during the closing months of 2017, it is unlikely that you are completely unfamiliar with Bitcoin. If you are like approximately 50 percent of the population, however, then you may not have a crystal-clear idea of what all of the fuss is about either. Luckily, this is a problem that is easily rectified; Bitcoin is a type of digital currency that can be used for all of the same things that traditional types of money can be used for. The only difference is that while traditional currencies are backed up by a third party (typically some type of government), Bitcoin's price is determined purely by what the market is willing to pay for it.

A trip in the way-back machine

Bitcoin, as it is known today, would not exist without an underlying technology known as blockchain. It is the Bitcoin blockchain that allows all of the Bitcoin transactions that are made each day, not only to be processed correctly but to be verified while remaining extremely secure at the same time. Even better, it all happens automatically. Blockchain technology, in turn, relies heavily on what is known as the proof of work model which is a concept that was developed in the 1990s to combat the then-new threat of email spam. The proof of work model requires a computer to complete a complicated mathematical equation before it can complete the task it was attempting, in this case sending an email. While completing one such equation was easy, completing enough to send a thousand or more emails at once was a non-starter.

While the technology never caught on in a big way at the time, it has since gone on to represent a key part of the way that blockchain technology can verify each transaction that ends up as a part of the blockchain. It essentially allows the Bitcoin blockchain to operate in a decentralized fashion without worrying about hackers not playing by the rules. This is the case because the information from individual transactions is collected into blocks, and before these blocks can be added to the blockchain they need to be verified through a process commonly referred to as Bitcoin mining.

This technology really took off in late 2008 on a P2P networking forum where a discussion was taking place regarding a digital currency that would have all the strengths of cash and none of its weaknesses. Most of the developers who were a part of the conversation saw it as little more than a thought experiment, but one person using the alias of Satoshi Nakamoto saw it as something far more. Soon after, the alias released a treatise on Bitcoin, while at the same time releasing the opensource code for blockchain technology and the Bitcoin blockchain as a proof of concept.

The Nakamoto alias then sent bitcoins to several of the other developers who were a part of the original conversation and mined the transaction, generating the first block in the blockchain. With this done, programmer interest around the new technology was piqued, and the Nakamoto alias faded into the background. Rumors persist, however, that the original Bitcoin wallet that Nakamoto used is still out there, waiting for someone to find it and take control of what could easily be a billion dollars' worth of Bitcoin.

At this point, bitcoins still were not worth anything because the market had not yet assigned any value to them, but this soon changed as one of the programmers soon traded 10,000 bitcoins to friend in exchange for two large pizzas, with a market value of about $20 placing the original value of a single bitcoin at about 0.02 cents. For the record, as of January 2017, one bitcoin was worth about $14,000, down from a high of about $20,000 in December.

Bitcoin transaction breakdown

Broadly speaking, you can think of the way a Bitcoin transaction works as operating the same as any PayPal transaction, the only difference is what is being transferred. In a more traditional online transaction, when the digital component is completed, the numbers being transferred between accounts have real-world analogs that are being counted, on a one to one basis. The amount in question will have a specific value that is unlikely to change anytime soon. On the other hand, with a Bitcoin transaction, there is nothing to the currency outside of the digital numbers, which means that the fiat value of the transaction could vary dramatically depending on when the party receiving the bitcoins choose to cash them out for a more traditional currency.

As noted previously, each transaction is then verified before being added to the blockchain proper. Once this is accomplished, it is then uploaded to all of the various nodes that are running the blockchain worldwide through an ease of use model that send the information from one node, to the next closest node, and so on and so forth until the information is everywhere. These nodes serve multiple key functions, the first of which is ensuring it is extremely unlikely for any of the information in the blockchain to be lost as all of the nodes would need to go down at once for this to be the case. The nodes also play a key role in security, however, as when a new block is added 51 percent of all the nodes need to verify that it is accurate for it to stick around.

To help keep everything straight, each block is provided with its own hash value, which is an alphanumeric value that relates to the information in the block specifically. This hash data then allows the blockchain to auto-sort as each hash also includes details regarding the block that proceeds the new block in the change. As such, it is impossible to change a block after the fact without also changing all of the blocks before it on the blockchain as well. This is another aspect of what keeps the blockchain so secure.

Understanding cryptocurrency pricing

Bitcoin is the most stable of all of the cryptocurrencies on the market today, and it still saw a fluctuation of about $6,000 in December alone. In fact, its volatility is such that it is expected to move about five percent each day. The average smaller cryptocurrency has that beat, however, and is known to move up to 15 percent each day. As such, this means that Bitcoin is still about three times as volatile as investing in gold and nearly five times more volatile than investing in any of the stocks on the S&P 500.

With greater risk comes greater reward. However, it then becomes a question of if the additional risk is worth it to you personally. For example, while a five percent positive movement in Bitcoin is not anything to write home about, that same five percent gain will likely represent all of the movement the S&P 500 stock might close out the entire year with. Likewise, it is not as if Bitcoin works on some magical pricing structure of its own; rather, it operates based on the same principals of supply and demand that all other markets do. In fact, as there is no guiding body to influence its price, many experts believe that cryptocurrencies actually reflect the purest reflection of supply and demand of any asset market.

This is not to say that geopolitical concerns do not affect the price of bitcoins, and, in fact, they are more prone to being affected by these types of concerns as they are not limited to specific areas of interest. For example, Bitcoin has previously seen serious movements in price as the result of events as varied as the devaluation of the yuan and the implementation of new capital controls in Greece.

Much of this movement is caused by speculative investors who can cause serious shifts in price by reacting to news, regardless of how that news would have affected Bitcoin in a vacuum. While Bitcoin was created to act as a functional, primarily transactional currency, like any more traditional currency, there are a few issues keeping this from being the case in practice. For starters, these issues are tied to the fact that there are currently far more Bitcoin users who are interested in buying and holding their bitcoins in hopes of future profits than there are who are interested in using it for its originally intended purpose. What's more, the issue is only magnified as the higher the price grows, the more it attracts investors and the less likely it is that people will buy it for its intended purpose.

Until the number of users grows to the point where its transactional value is too great to ignore, Bitcoin will continue to exist in what is known as a pricing bubble. This bubble is the physical representation of the difference between the price that the market feels that Bitcoin is currently worth and the price that it is currently trading for. As mass adoption rates increase, this will eventually lead to a point of mass saturation where more people are finally using the cryptocurrency for its desired purpose than the speculative demand can keep up with. This will ultimately lead to a serious devaluation of the currency until it is more in line with its practical value.

This is not to say that pricing bubbles are inherently bad. However, it is just to note that it is important to approach them cautiously to ensure that you will benefit from them, as opposed to getting in too late and risking losing out on all your potential profits as a result. Bitcoin pricing bubbles are typically influenced by the following:

Media:

The leading cause of dramatic bubble increases come as a result of the media reporting on a given cryptocurrency. It was true about Bitcoin when the price broke $1,000 for the first time and it remained true in December of 2017 when it reached its current overall high as well. It does not matter what facet of the cryptocurrency they are covering, simply hearing about how a specific investment is especially hot right now is always going to be enough to get new people to jump on board without fully thinking things through first. Unsurprisingly, this can lead to miniature bubbles forming on top of the overall bubble that burst more quickly due to natural market movement.

The media tends to focus on stories that relate to a cryptocurrency being added to a new exchange or when it experiences an upgrade that will allow it to serve either more users or existing users more effectively. Additionally, they will be perennially interested in anything that can be cropped into a good soundbite or stories that prove the cryptocurrency market is expanding in the way they are already reporting it is. Overall, the specific context of the content is not going to be nearly as important as the coverage itself, even negative content can actually increase the price as people buy in at what they assume is a bargain price.

Public opinion:

Every cryptocurrency has a dedicated fanbase and Bitcoin is no different. These individuals are those who can be thought of as the true believers, and they are especially useful when it comes to spreading the word and making others believe in the possibilities associated with cryptocurrency as a whole. The more effort these types of individuals put into getting the rest of the world to believe that a given cryptocurrency is a viable alternative, the more they are to actually convert others to their way of thinking. These people are also known to provide valuable feedback to programmers, do work on the code themselves and, of course, invest heavily in it with their own money. Each of these helps to drive the price of the cryptocurrency even higher.

The best example of these types of advocates in action can be

seen during the 2014 Bitcoin pricing explosion. This was the

point where the cryptocurrency was first reaching the

mainstream while still struggling to become more than just a way for college kids to buy drugs online. With the help of these advocates, the overall interest in the cryptocurrency peaked enough to eventually send the price over $1,000 per Bitcoin, a positive trajectory that has been maintained ever since.

Online scuttlebutt:

When news regarding a fiat currency breaks, it is a safe bet that traditional media is doing the breaking. When news about Bitcoin breaks, however, it will be social media of one type or another that will catch the news first. There are countless social media groups out there dedicated to cryptocurrency of all time, and Bitcoin, as the king of the roost has more than anyone else. Members of these groups are not exactly middle of the road when it comes to Bitcoin, which means that any positive rumor that gets out there is likely to fuel a price increase, regardless of whether or not the rumor is substantiated, which becomes irrelevant after the sudden price boost slows down and anyone stops to think what generated it in the first place.

Chapter 2: Getting Started with Bitcoin

Choosing a wallet

Before you can do anything with Bitcoin whatsoever, the first thing you will need to do is find a reliable, and secure, Bitcoin wallet. As the bitcoins that you purchase will not have any sort of physical representation, choosing a trustworthy wallet is crucial to ensuring you retain control of your bitcoins in the long-term. Despite the name, a Bitcoin wallet does not actually store your bitcoins; rather, it stores a pair of addresses which correspond to where your bitcoins are kept in the chain. One address will be public and will be shared to complete all of your Bitcoin transactions, and the other will be private, and you will want to keep it that way as it provides complete access to your Bitcoin account. Anyone with access to your private address can do anything with your bitcoins they desire which is why it is important to keep it safe.

Broadly speaking, there are two types of Bitcoin wallets, hot and cold. Hot wallets are less secure than cold wallets because they are directly connected to the internet which makes them far more vulnerable to all sorts of malicious activity. Hot wallets are the easiest type of wallet to use, and most people maintain both a hot wallet and a cold wallet, the first for their daily transactions and the second for their long-term investments.

Hot wallets come in two types, online and software. Online wallets keep the relevant wallet addresses stored in one large database which means these are the wallets that hackers will target first as a result. They can be accessed from any device that runs a web browser. Software wallets are downloaded directly onto either a computer or smart device and can thus be accessed even if the device in question is not directly connected to the internet at the moment.

Cold wallets also come in several different varieties, each of which deals with the inherent insecurity of hot wallets in different ways. First, there is the hardware wallet, the most commonly used type of cold wallet on the market today. This type of wallet is essentially an encrypted USB drive with a screen that allows the user to interface with their bitcoins directly. It is designed in such a way that it is impossible to get to the address details in a usable form without the

relevant password being in place.

Another option that is both more cost-effective and more

secure, if a little more cumbersome is known as a paper

wallet. When set up properly, this type of wallet is virtually

impossible to trace back to you and, indeed, the only proof of

ownership you will have is a printed out QR code that links

to your private wallet directly. To create this type of wallet,

all you need to do is visit WalletGenerator.net, before then

visiting the link it directs you to on GitHub to download the

files for the website.

With the files obtained, you will then want to run all of the

virus software at your disposal before then disconnecting

from the internet completely. With this done, you will then

want to open the page you downloaded and then follow the

instructions for generating the paper wallet. All that is left to do is print off both QR codes, the public key and the private key, before deleting all trace of the website from your computer. Finally, all you need to do is take a picture of your public key QR code and store your private QR code someplace safe.

An even more secure type of cold wallet is known as a mind wallet which creates a URL to a specific wallet location based on a 12-word passphrase that you need to enter at BitAddress.org to gain access to the private key associated with the passphrase. As long as you do not write down the passphrase that you use, there is literally no way for anyone to trace the wallet to you, or to even prove that the wallet exists. With this type of wallet, it is important that you do not store anything in it until you have proven to yourself sufficiently that you will not forget it.

Buying your first Bitcoin

While you will certainly want to look into the right type of cold wallet for you, at some point in the future, the best way to get your feet wet with bitcoins is by using the Coinbase Copay wallet which is available for virtually all platforms from Coinbase.com. This is a software wallet, but it should be plenty secure for your initial forays into Bitcoin. As such, to get started all you will need to do is download the app and then sign up for an account.

Once you have verified your identity, you will then be able to access your account page which should look similar to the one you use for online banking. From this point, all that will be left is to select the option to buy, then select how you wish to go about doing so, and confirming the transaction. You will then receive your first bitcoins, typically in less than an hour. Keep in mind that what you receive will not be one to one, however, as there will be fees that need to be paid for the transaction that will affect the number of bitcoins you ultimately end up with.

While the interface may seem pretty straightforward, the truth of the matter is that you are not so much purchasing bitcoins with a fiat currency directly, so much as you are placing a buy order on the Coinbase exchange and then being automatically paired up with a seller who is willing to sell for the price at which you were quoted. While Coinbase is a well-regarded exchange, when you start branching out into other wallet options it is important to ensure that things are on the level before putting all of your bitcoins someplace you end up regretting later.

Exchange considerations

When it comes to looking into various exchanges, you will notice they all have different fees, and even different going rates for the same types of cryptocurrency. This is because all cryptocurrency exchanges are unregulated and unaffiliated with one another which makes each essentially an island unto itself. While this means there are certainly plenty of different strategies for taking advantage of such things, discussed in later chapters, it also means that you need to be especially choosy as there is not going to be anyone to turn to if the exchange you choose folds overnight, taking your bitcoins with it.

The best place to start will be looking at what other users think about the exchange you are considering and the best place to find reviews of such things will be on the Bitcoin subreddit page. When looking into what other people have to say about a specific exchange, you do not need to avoid exchanges with any negative comments, just those with negative comments that all suggest the same general theme. If three or four people report having the same problem, it is probably not that much of an issue, but if 30 or 40 do, then it is probably best to steer clear, just in case.

Once you have weeded out the worst of the worst, the next thing you will want to do is make sure the exchange you are working with is as transparent as can be expected. Each exchange works off an order book which keeps track of all of the transactions that the exchange has been a part of since it came online. Having access to an exchange's order book will make it easier to ensure that they are not hiding anything and will also allow you to confirm that their available funds are enough to cover all of their debts. If this is not the case, then the exchange is what is known as a fractional exchange, and it should be avoided at all costs. If enough people try to pull all of their funds from the exchange all at once, it will be unable to make good on its debts and thus will have no choice but to fold.

It is also important to ensure that the exchange you are considering will be as secure as possible. For starters, this means that their URL starts with HTTPS, not HTTP as this indicates that they are using a secure protocol when they transmit data. Additionally, you will want to ensure that you can set up some sort of dual-factor authentication to make it, so you have to do more than simply enter a password to gain access to your account.

Assuming security is on the level, you will then need to consider the types of fees that the exchange charges on top of the fee that the Bitcoin blockchain charges for each transaction. If you plan on purchasing large numbers of Bitcoin all at once, then you will want to find an exchange that charges a flat fee per transaction. While this amount is typically going to be higher than it otherwise might be, it will still end up costing you less in the long run. On the other hand, if you plan on executing a large number of trades that are smaller overall, then you will want to find an exchange that charges a percentage of the transaction total when it comes to fees.

Likewise, you will want to ensure that the exchange you choose will always lock in the price you will pay at the moment that the trade is initiated as opposed to when it is processed. As Bitcoin transactions can frequently take dramatically different amounts of time to process, moving forward with an exchange where this is not the case can lead to prices that have changed dramatically between initiation and completion, turning an easy profit into a loss which you are completely unable to derail.

Finally, whenever possible, it is important to try and choose a local exchange above all others. Doing so is beneficial for several reasons, the first of which is that it will help to ensure that you can trade during peak times more easily, naturally leading to larger profits as a result. Additionally, while still far from guaranteed, investing in a local exchange will make it somewhat more likely that you will be able to receive some assistance if the exchange does, in fact, end up going belly up. While it is still not a guarantee, being able to talk to someone local about the issue dramatically increases the probability of the issue being resolved.

Chapter 3: Bitcoin Investing

One of the best things about getting started investing in Bitcoin is that a lack of previous investment experience does not hinder you nearly as much as it might in other markets, simply because a vast majority of investors are in the same position, as the market is still so new. Additionally, due to the high level of volatility involved in the market, one of the most reliable investment strategies to pursue, the buy and hold strategy, is also one of the simplest.

To get started with a buy and hold strategy, all you need to do is wait until the price drops to at or near its current low and then use that as your entry point to hold onto the bitcoins until they reach a price that is near their current high. With the profits you make, you then wait for the price to drop again and buy back in, repeating the process as needed to ensure that the number of bitcoins you can accumulate will then likely be able to accrue enough value in the long-term to meet your investment goals.

Taking these steps will allow you to take full advantage of the concept of compounding, which is crucial to maximizing your investments in the long run while also minimizing the downsides that come along with investing in Bitcoin, primarily the extreme amount of risk. The basic idea behind compounding is that reinvesting your early returns is the best, and most effective, means of maximizing your profits in the long run. Selling when the price is high and then buying it again when it has dropped allows you to do just that.

To fully understand the potential that compounding offers, all you need to do is consider the example of the average 25-year-old who is looking to retire as a millionaire by the time they are 65. To do this successfully, they will need to save an average of $900 per month, each month, until they retire, assuming they are seeing a very modest five percent return, per year, on their investment. However, if they waited just 10 years until they were 35 to start saving, then they would need to save about $2,200 each month to reach their goal. Likewise, if they waited to start saving seriously until they were 45, then they would need to save around $4,500 each month to see the same results.

While long-term investment plans generally make do with reliable, but minimal year-over-year returns, Bitcoin's volatility means that, depending on when you invest, you could easily see a decade or more's worth of growth in a year, at least in the relatively near future. While these extreme pricing jags will naturally decrease over time as the price the market is willing to pay, and the price speculators have driven the price to, come more in line with one another. As such, when it comes to investing in Bitcoin, there may very well never be a better time to do so.

While getting started quickly is key to maximizing your profits, this does not mean that you should jump in head first without stopping to think about what your personal investment habits are like to ensure that they end up helping, rather than hurting, your overall investment potential. As such, when you are first starting out, the first thing you should keep in mind is that not all investing strategies will be right for every individual and the biggest determining factor is always going to be the level of risk that you will be comfortable with. While cryptocurrency is naturally riskier than a vast majority of other investments, this does not mean that there are not still some shades of gray to consider on the topic.

Determining your true level of ideal risk should start with an honest assessment of the goals you have for the money you ultimately invest. If you are more risk averse, as a rule, then you may be happy with the goal of keeping as much of your initial investment capital intact as possible. On the other hand, if you are not afraid of pushing your risk to the limit then your goal could be maximum profit regardless of the risk. Remember, when it comes to investing successfully, there is no risk without reward, and if a greater risk does not come with a comparably greater reward, then it likely is not worth considering.

The specifics of the plan you choose are not going to be nearly as important as the fact that after you decide as to how you will move forward, you stick to it no matter what. When an unexpected loss comes along to snatch defeat from the jaws of success, it can be easy to want to go against again your plan and do something rash in an effort to regain lost profits; this is a negative habit to get into, however, and it will always lead to additional losses as opposed to profits. When you are putting your plan together, it is also important to keep in mind that your goals will not be completed in a vacuum, taking into account the challenges you will need to overcome them will make it far easier for you to overcome them successfully.

When creating a plan, the entire point is to use to make yourself as mechanical and logical in your investments as possible. Emotion is the enemy of logic, and giving into it will always cause you see fewer profits than you otherwise would. A big part of keeping your emotions in check will be ensuring that you never invest more money than you would be able to realistically afford to lose. If you spend your time worrying that you will lose money that you need to survive, then there is no way you will be able to avoid the emotional pull to keep those funds safe, even if it runs counter to what your plan says to do.

When it comes to considering the right amount of risk to face on a regular basis, as a general rule, the longer you have until you plan on using your investment funds, the greater the amount of risk you can successfully take on at the moment as you have enough time to bounce back from any serious losses that come about as a result. All told, if you are planning to invest for 10 years or more, then there is no reason you should not lean as hard on potential risks as you possibly can.

Tips for investment success

Investing in Bitcoin successfully is a skill, which means like any other it is only likely to improve with practice. To speed things up somewhat, consider the following tips:

Always treat it like a commodity:

While there is so much speculative interest around Bitcoin these days, it is easy to forget that it is actually just a commodity, which means it is subject to many of the same rules as any other commodity. Just like commodities such as precious or base metals, bitcoins are used for both speculative and practical purposes. As such, if you are interested in tracking the likely movement of Bitcoin in either the short or long-term, the easiest way to do so is to look for ways that Bitcoin is increasing its practical value as opposed to its speculative value. This means taking a look at the aspects of the service that people are talking about and ensuring that public opinion (non-speculative, of course) remains strong. In the long run, what speculators think does not matter nearly as much as what the market believes the price will be worth.

Keep an eye on saturation levels:

While Bitcoin is currently operating under a sustained pricing bubble, it is unlikely that it will burst seriously, anytime soon. As such, there is still plenty of time to get in and make a profit, at virtually any pricing point, as long as you are in a strong overall position when the mass saturation level reaches a point where it could tip over at any moment. When this occurs, it will be important to keep a close eye on what analysts believe the true market value of the cryptocurrency is. If your investments were made at above this level, then you may be better off selling early as opposed to holding out to the last moment to maximize profits that may vanish if you are not careful.

This mass saturation point is anticipated to take place sometime in 2022, though the date could move forward if unanticipated leaps are made either in the technology itself or its adoption for one reason or another. This point will become closer and closer as new and improved ways of interacting with cryptocurrency are introduced to the public, and they learn about the many ways it and blockchain technology can influence their lives for the better.

Know where you are in the market cycle:

All markets and all assets move through the same cyclical pattern when given a long enough timeframe which is what makes it so useful when it comes to pinpointing the current state of the cycle. The market cycle typically becomes noticeable when an asset reaches a state of stable growth that causes the market as a whole to feel optimistic about its potential. This naturally causes the price to rise even higher, which causes the price to rise to points that are ultimately unsustainable thanks to euphoric investor speculation.

The state of euphoria will likely continue until the first shades of anxiety start to show as the bubble bursts and the price drops. This drop is then typically followed by a brief reprieve because investors refuse to believe what is happening right in front of them. This denial ultimately costs them, however, as the downward spiral is only starting, and the price will continue to drop as the market moves from a period of fear to one of depression regarding the asset's prospects. When the point of no return is reached, panic is sure to set in, and the price will continue to decrease until it reaches its lowest low.

With the price now once again completely in line with what the market believes it to be worth, which will make it possible for it to begin to rise once more. This will, in turn, cause investors confidence to rise from panic, back through depression and eventually to hope for the future. Once hope sets in it is only a matter of time before the market as a whole takes notice and things become optimistic once more.

Bitcoin has already been through the entire process once, finishing up with the crash of 2014. If the state of growth at the end of 2017 marked the start of the next true phase of optimism, or if it actually marks the start of the euphoric phase, it is too soon to say. It is definitely something for investors who are just getting in now to consider, however, and worth keeping an eye out for the mass saturation point as well.

While Bitcoin is likely strong enough to survive any type of crash at this point, the next crash in price is likely going to take down a vast majority of the cryptocurrencies out there, more than 1,000 in all, in a purge akin to what happened after the dotcom bubble burst in the late 90s. Experts estimate that as little as 20 percent of the cryptocurrencies currently in operation will survive the mass saturation transition.

Plan for the long-term:

While the growth Bitcoin experienced in 2017 turned many people into millionaires virtually overnight, it is important that you not start investing in Bitcoin with the goal of quitting your day job within a year's time. While the 2017 price explosion was not the first time the price of a Bitcoin has jumped substantially, virtually overnight, this in no way makes it anything but the exception to the rule. For each of the major pricing jumps, the price has stayed somewhat stable for years at a time.

This, in turn, means that you will need to approach investing in Bitcoin with the right mindset to hope to see sufficient results. Starting out with expectations that are completely unrealistic are only going to make it more difficult for you to stick to your plan no matter what and keep your emotions out of the equation entirely. Failing to do so can lead to a wide variety of potential issues that will make it difficult, if not impossible, to reach your long-term goals.

While a vast majority of long-term investment options have additional lock-in risk associated with holding on to them in the long-term, this is one facet of investing in Bitcoin that is actually less risky than the alternative. This is because unloading your bitcoins is as easy as going to any exchange and converting them back into cash. What's more, you can choose virtually any exchange that has the highest current rate as if you already have bitcoins in hand; most exchanges do not even require that you verify your identity before you are allowed to start trading. All told, this makes it easy to think of your cold Bitcoin wallet as a type of savings account with an extremely high return on investment.

Cloud mining

Cloud mining is another type of long-term Bitcoin investment option. In this case, you would pay a cloud mining service to mine bitcoins for you, and then keep the profits as a result. If you do not have a significant amount of capital saved for investment purposes, this is a viable alternative as each transaction that is mined generates a small amount of Bitcoin for the miner. Cloud mining works by sharing processing power as a means of running data centers remotely that take care of the actual mining. In this type of scenario, you do not need anything special other than a Bitcoin wallet, and a way to contact the cloud mining company you are considering.

Cloud mining does come with additional risks, however, starting with the fact that many cloud mining services out there are currently scams, operating a variation of a traditional Ponzi Scheme. The best place to go when it comes to finding a legitimate cloud mining service will be the Bitcoin subreddit. Once you know the mining service is on the level, you are also going to want to be careful to read the contract closely, as some cloud mining services will require a certain commitment up front, and other will shut down if the price of Bitcoin drops below a certain point. Knowing just what you are getting into is the best way to ensure that the process will end up being profitable for you in the long-term.

All told, there are three main types of cloud mining services, the first of which, hosted mining, leases out entire mining machines and lets users collect the profits. The next, virtual hosted mining, creates virtual mining machines that run a portion of a machine's full power; inside these virtual machines, the user has complete control to mine in whatever way they see fit. The cheapest starter option is typically to lease a portion of a machine's hashing power and then generate profits based on what that hashing power provides.

Chapter 4: Bitcoin Trading

To trade Bitcoin successfully in the short-term, it is important that you create a personalized trading plan, just as if you were investing in a long-term strategy instead. Additionally, however, when it comes to determining your tolerance for risk, you will want to factor in the level of returns you are looking for to ensure that the time you spend trading is worth what you are likely to get back. Unlike with investing, trading Bitcoin successfully means being willing and able to devote time to the practice, actively, on a regular basis.

The fewer hours each day you have available to devote to trading, the more you will need to be willing to risk with each trade to see larger returns. If this does not sound good to you, then you will either need to put in more time in general, or lower your expectations, as these are the only things about the equation that can be changed. In general, you are only going to want to commit to trades that you expect to net you a 300 percent return on investment. Likewise, a good rule of thumb is to never put more than 5 percent of your total trading capital into any single trade to prevent serious losses and ensure you always live to trade another day.

Additionally, it is very important to not start trading without a general idea of what you expect the entry and exit points to be. Knowing when you will be willing to walk with your profits, and also when you are willing to cut your losses and walk away, is crucial to your long-term success. This will also make it easier to ignore the urge to squeeze every single cent out of an already profitable trade which is good because it is only going to lead to greater losses in the long-term.

The exit point that makes the most sense for you will be tailored to your tolerance for risk which means you are never going to change it once you are committed to the trade, as from that point on emotions could easily be keeping you from thinking clearly. As such, the exit point that you decide on should then be determined ahead of time-based on your level of risk tolerance and the length of time you plan on holding your trades in general.

Likewise, when it comes to choosing profitable entry points, you will want to seek out those that most naturally align with your predetermined risk level as opposed to those that go against your natural tendencies, regardless of whether they seem as though they might be profitable. If you have to worry about fighting your natural tendencies, then you will not be fully focused on the trade and far more likely to make a mistake.

This is why it is extremely important to set daily trading limits, especially as a new trader, to protect you from making a series of losing trades that you are only going to regret later. Setting a strict amount of losses that you can accept in a single day before calling it quits will not only serve to ensure that a single bad day does not ruin you, it will also help to ensure that your emotions do not have an opportunity to turn small losses into larger ones by not giving yourself time to take a breather and ensure the loss is not affecting you. A good rule of thumb is to limit yourself to a loss of 10 percent of your trading capital, per day, at least until you have become more comfortable with this type of inevitable loss.

Finally, while the strategies outlined in the following pages can make it easier to pinpoint existing trends, and take advantage of them appropriately, it is important to never forget that supply and demand are at the heart of all Bitcoin pricing movements. Keeping this in mind will often make it easier to cut through the clutter and false noise that surrounds pricing movement and help you focus on the heart of the matter.

As a general rule, if the supply is currently low then prices will naturally be higher as a result which means that it is time to sell while the lack of demand remains. Meanwhile, if demand is high, then prices will be low, and it will be a great time to pick up some extra bitcoins on the cheap. This does not mean you are not going to want to focus on more complex methods of determining trends, it just means you should never neglect to consider the fundamentals as well.

Continuation patterns

If you have ever found yourself looking at Bitcoin's pricing movement only to be unable to see a pattern, then it could be that you simply are not looking at things in the right way. In fact, the geometric patterns that can often be found in this type of price data will frequently allow the entire pricing movement into focus. These shapes are generally indicative of what are known as continuation patterns which indicate that the related pricing trend is likely going to continue in the current direction.

These types of patterns tend to occur most frequently in the middle of existing trends and tend to manifest as a pause in the primary price action for a varying degree of time. When these types of patterns typically make themselves visible, it indicates that the trend is likely to resume and continue for the rest of its duration. A pattern can be considered finished after it has formed completely and a breakout has occurred, which may not have been directly related to the trend in the first place. With practice, you should be able to easily pick out continuation patterns at practically any time frame. Common patterns to watch for include flags, rectangles, triangles, and pennants.

These types of patterns can prove exceedingly useful when it comes to providing logic to seemingly random data. Knowing the patterns to be on the lookout for means that you will be able to create a more reliable trading plan, in turn, that will make it possible to take advantage of them in ways that may not be visible when using other methods. It is important to understand. However, that continuation patterns are not going to be reliable across the board, they can still be impaired by unexpected trend reversals.

Additionally, it is possible that the bounds of the pattern could be met, but not broken through completely, and the pattern could still be considered completed. This is known as a false breakout, and it could occur several times before a true breakout occurs, and a new pattern starts. Rectangles are the most susceptible to this type of movement as they are the easiest to spot and are the most frequently used by new traders.

The most reliable pattern that you will want to be on the lookout for is the triangle. This pattern typically occurs when the price range converges with naturally lower highs along with higher than average lows. When the convergence reaches its highest point, the price action then creates a triangle formation. You will likely find triangles that are ascending, symmetrical and descending, but they can all be traded in the same basic way.

Triangle patterns are not likely to stick around for any set period of time. Instead, you will want to be on the lookout for a minimum of two high price points as well as two corresponding low-price swings. As the price continues to converge, it will ultimately reach an apex, the point of the triangle, and the closer this is to occur, the tighter the price action becomes and the more likely it is that a breakout will occur.

The flag continuation pattern will occur during prominently placed pauses during long-standing trends. They most often occur when the price ends up being confined to a small range that exists between parallel lines. Flags such as these typically only stick around for a short length of time, no more than a handful of bars at most. Additionally, they are easy to spot because they do not contain the type of price swings that tend to mark trending ranges or channels that are well-defined. Flags can form parallel to one another or in a slopping fashion, either up or down.

Pennant patterns often form in ways that look quite similar to triangles if you are not paying close enough attention.

They tend to be smaller than triangles, however, and will always contain less than 20 bars, anything more and you would be looking at a triangle. Pennant tends to form when the price converges to cover an average price range that appears in the middle of a larger trend to generate the pennant appearance.

Arbitrage

While the fact that no two cryptocurrency exchanges are directly connected was briefly discussed in a previous chapter, what this means for the crafty trader was only hinted at. The truth of the matter is the lack of interconnectivity among various exchanges means that it is often possible to find Bitcoin trading at prices at prices that differ by $100 or more. Due to the amount of volatility inherent in the market, these types of differences materialize every day. As an example, on the day that the price of a single Bitcoin rose above $10,000 for the first time, there were several hours where it was trading above $10,000 in exchanges in South Korea while trading for about $9,750 on most US exchanges.

This example highlights just how fruitful the arbitrage opportunities that Bitcoin presents currently are. This will remain the case for as long as the market remains unregulated, varied and disjointed. While a price gap of the levels that Bitcoin regularly sees would be closed quickly in a more connected market, the fact that the disparities here are spread out among such a vast array of exchanges, coupled with the sheer speed at which the price can change means that any type of immediate correction is practically impossible unless the discrepancy shows up within a single exchange.

Additionally worth taking note of is the fact that a majority of those looking for arbitrage opportunities in the cryptocurrency market these days are not professional, though institutional investors are already starting to sniff around the gates. As such, the best time to take advantage of these types of differences will be sooner rather than later before interest from this sector swoops in and forces all the personal traders to fight over the scraps. For example, trading institution Goldman Sachs plans to have Bitcoin trading desk set up by fall 2018 and other major trading groups are sure to follow suit. This means that institutional traders are certainly coming, it is not a question of if but when.

One of the most commonly used types of arbitrage when it comes to taking advantage of cryptocurrency's unique complexities is what is known as triangular arbitrage which actually involves making multiple trades between three different currencies, or cryptocurrencies, as the case may be. When done correctly, this will practically ensure that you make a profit off two of the trades and guarantees that you will make a profit on at least one of them. What's more, with practice you will find opportunities to use it virtually every single day.

When taking advantage of this strategy, you will want to start by being on the lookout for situations where a specific currency is being overvalued when compared to one of the other currencies while still being undervalued when compared to the third. From there you will then want to determine the cross rate and the implied cross rate. Assuming the anticipated difference is found, then the first cryptocurrency will be traded for the second. When done correctly this will allow for risk-free profit as long as the proper imbalances are maintained. You will then trade the third cryptocurrency for the first, netting another round of profit by doing so.

To decide if a particular opportunity for arbitrage exists, you will want to use this equation: $(A/B \times B/C \times C/A = 1)$. Here, A will be the current rate of the first cryptocurrency, and B and C will be the rates for the other two. If the equation above works out to something other than a total of 1, then you have the opportunity to profit from triangular arbitrage.

Locking in profit through triangular arbitrage means that there is no further chance of market risk coming in an interfering with your profits. Other types of risk do remain, however, the biggest of which is counterparty risk. This would only occur if one part of the transaction failed to go through, such as if the block its transaction in was orphaned. The best way to mitigate this risk is by executing all three legs of the triangular arbitrage maneuver as possible. Before doing so, of course, it is also important to factor in various transaction fees that will be accrued across all three transactions to ensure that things end up working out as profitably as anticipated.

Conclusion

Thank you for making it through to the end of *Bitcoin: Best Strategies for Investing and Profiting from Bitcoin*, let's hope it was informative and able to provide you with all of the tools you need to achieve your goals, whatever it is that they may be. Just because you've finished this book does not mean there is nothing left to learn on the topic, expanding your horizons is the only way to find the mastery you seek.

Remember, for all the cultural cache that Bitcoin has at the moment, the fact of the matter is that it is still an extremely new technology which means that dedicating yourself to the study of the market is the only way to see reliable results in the long-term. As such, after you start investing or trading, resting on your laurels is only going to see you losing out in the long-term to those who were better informed. Keep it up, and you will need a Bitcoin money bin to keep all of your bitcoins in.

Likewise, it is extremely important to take your time when creating your personalized trading plan. While it is also important to not wait too long to take full advantage of the potential for profit Bitcoin offers, there is nothing to be gained by jumping in early without a firm idea of what you hope to accomplish. Taking a slow and thoughtful approach will allow you to maximize the advantages you do have, leading to better overall profits in the process. This is not to say that the going will be easy, however, as the volatility in play means nothing is certain. One thing you can count on, however, is that making money from Bitcoin is a marathon, not a sprint, which means that slow and steady wins the race.

Remember though, it is not always sunshine and rainbow. There may be storms along the way. The point is, Bitcoin can help you earn profit but it is not always a guarantee. So, before investing, gather enough information, learn the ins and outs, study the advantages and disadvantages of investing in Bitcoin, and analyze the common mistakes that many make. Doing so can help you avoid the risk of losing your money.

Finally, if you found this book useful in any way, a review on Amazon is always appreciated!

www.ingramcontent.com/pod-product-compliance
Lightning Source LLC
Chambersburg PA
CBHW071228220526
45468CB00002B/771